BEHIND YOU!

Paul Cookson and **David Harmer** have known each other since the Loch Ness Monster was a tadpole and Grendel was a baby monster with no teeth at all but very tough gums. They work individually in schools, libraries, front rooms, tents, village halls and the depths of many a monster's lair as poets and workshop leaders, or they perform together as Spill the Beans, entertaining hundreds of little monsters and their parents with a fast-paced, dazzling poetry show. Between them they have published a monstrous number of books and right now they are behind you. Watch out!

PS The only things they're frightened of are dinner ladies and diets.

Paul's website is: www.paulcooksonpoet.co.uk
David's website is: www.davidharmer.com

Carl Flint lives in Sheffield with Emma, Oscar and Lily Grace. He has worked in comics, magazines, newspapers and TV on everything from *Sonic the Hedgehog* and Nickelodeon to Channel 4 adverts and Swedish ice-cream commercials. He likes cake but is scared of meringue. Spooky!

Carl's website is: www.carlflint.com

IT'S BEHIND YOU!

MONSTER POEMS BY
PAUL COOKSON AND DAVID HARMER

Illustrated by Carl Flint

MACMILLAN CHILDREN'S BOOKS

First published 2010 by Macmillan Children's Books

This edition published 2013 by Macmillan Children's Books
a division of Macmillan Publishers Limited
20 New Wharf Road, London N1 9RR
Basingstoke and Oxford
Associated companies throughout the world
www.panmacmillan.com

ISBN 978-1-4472-4210-9

1 3 5 7 9 8 6 4 2

A CIP catalogue record for this book is available from
the British Library.

Printed and bound by CPI Group (UK) Ltd, Croydon CR0 4YY

To Sam, Daisy, Lizzie, Harriet, Oscar and Lily,
our favourite monsters

Contents

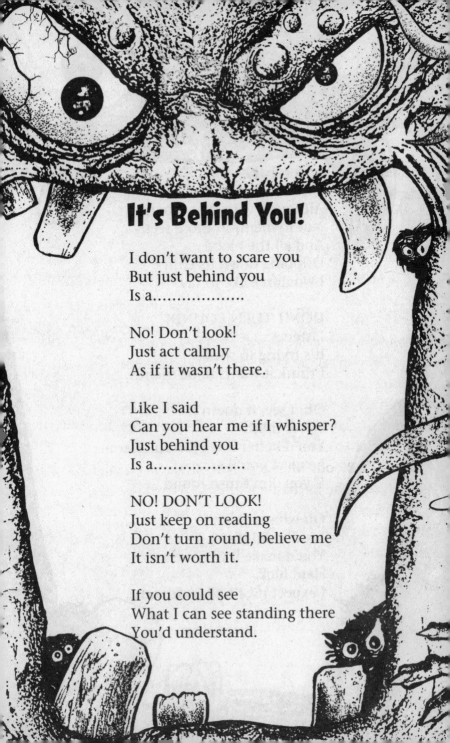

It's Behind You!

I don't want to scare you
But just behind you
Is a....................

No! Don't look!
Just act calmly
As if it wasn't there.

Like I said
Can you hear me if I whisper?
Just behind you
Is a....................

NO! DON'T LOOK!
Just keep on reading
Don't turn round, believe me
It isn't worth it.

If you could see
What I can see standing there
You'd understand.

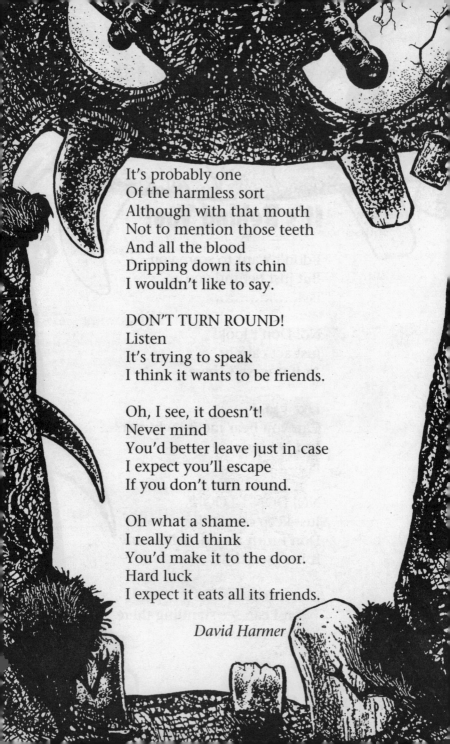

It's probably one
Of the harmless sort
Although with that mouth
Not to mention those teeth
And all the blood
Dripping down its chin
I wouldn't like to say.

DON'T TURN ROUND!
Listen
It's trying to speak
I think it wants to be friends.

Oh, I see, it doesn't!
Never mind
You'd better leave just in case
I expect you'll escape
If you don't turn round.

Oh what a shame.
I really did think
You'd make it to the door.
Hard luck
I expect it eats all its friends.

David Harmer

Worse Than Half a Maggot

They say that finding half a maggot in your apple
is worse than finding a whole maggot.

That's not true.

Finding an alien vampire caterpillar with
    poisonous fangs
razor spikes and a lightning laser-beam tongue

is much, much worse.

Paul Cookson

We Are Not Alone

When the floorboards creak and hinges squeak
When the TV's off but seems to speak
When the moon is full and you hear a shriek
We are not alone

When the spiders gather beneath your bed
When they colonize the garden shed
When they spin their webs right above your head
We are not alone

When the lights are out and there's no one home
When you're by yourself and you're on your own
When the radiators bubble and groan
We are not alone

When the shadows lengthen round your wall
When you hear deep-breathing in the hall
When you think there's no one there at all
We are not alone

When the branches tap on your window-pane
When the finger twigs scritch scratch again
When something's changed but it looks the same
We are not alone

When the wallpaper is full of eyes
When the toys in the dark all change in size
When anything's a monster in disguise
We are not alone

You'd better watch out whatever you do
There's something out there looking at you
When you think you're on your own
We are not
      We are not
           We are not alone

Paul Cookson

I'm Right Here

I'm the dream
You didn't want to have
The nightmare driving you mad.

I'm the monster
In the bushes in the park
The footsteps ringing after dark.

I'm the vampire
Flapping round your room
The darkness, shadow and gloom.

I'm the Nasty
The Horrid and the Spite
The hairy, scary feeling in the night.

I'm the reeking, speaking, stomach tweaking
Staircase creaking whilst you're sleeping
Creeping so your heart is leaping
Thing.

I'll sing
My werewolf song
Bring along my friend King Kong.

My bones
Will rattle your ears
My moans and groans will stir your fears.

What's that?
Well, they are mine
Those tingling fingers down your spine.

Don't scream
Don't make a sound
I'm right here, don't turn round!

David Harmer

Grizelda Grimm's Ghastly Gun

I've built a giant ray gun
And when I beam it down
Nasty things will happen
To the children in your town.

I'll puncture all their footballs
Ruin all their games
Make sure they fight and scrap and kick
Call each other names
I'll blow up their PlayStations
With my wicked beam
I'll burn their burgers, zap their chocolates
Melt their fresh ice cream
My ghastly gun will trash their toys
Cut their bikes in half
As their computers all explode
You'll hear my evil laugh
Each time they try to chomp some gum
Or chew some greasy chips
My rays will blast out super-fast
And superglue their lips
When they feel sick I'll get a kick
To watch them wail and cry
As I torch their teddies
And their MP3s all fry.

I think I'll start tomorrow
Make my wicked dreams come true
I'm going to mess up everything
There's nothing you can do

Creating stacks of chaos
Is just my kind of fun
Yes I'm Grizelda Grimm
With my ghoulish, ghastly gun.

David Harmer

Little Foot Big Foot

I'm a little foot Big Foot
I may be very hairy
Because my feet are tiny
I'm not very scary

Paul Cookson

The Finger in the Biscuit Tin

Feeling somewhat peckish
I stuffed my hand right in
But nothing could prepare me for
The finger in the biscuit tin

It wasn't made from chocolate
But it was long and thin
Lurking with the Jaffa Cakes
The finger in the biscuit tin

Custard Creams don't have nails
Digestives don't have skin
Bourbons don't have bones like
The finger in the biscuit tin

The glisten of the gristle
The tendon stretched and slim
The bending of the joints of
The finger in the biscuit tin

What to do when hunger strikes?
So with an evil grin
I picked, licked, crunched, munched
The finger from the biscuit tin

Paul Cookson

The Football Field Foul Fiend

Fifty foot of fearful fur
Fiendish feral fungus fangs
Fast ferocious freaky fins
The football field foul fiend

Fiery furnace furious features
Frightening frightful phantom face
Filthy fouling fearsome feet
The football field foul fiend

Paul Cookson

Whispers Outside the Graveyard

Where are we going? *Into the graveyard.*
Why are we going? *Wait and see.*
When are we going? *Round about midnight.*
Who will be going? *Just you and me.*

Who will I see there? *Zombies playing.*

Why are we going? *For some fun.*

What if I don't want to? *Well, you have to.*

What's that moaning? *The fun has begun!*

What if it's scary? *Well, it will be.*
Very very scary? *Yes, that's right.*
Really scary zombies? *At least two hundred.*
When will I come home? *Not tonight.*

Not tonight? *That's right*
Nobody at all
Goes home tonight!

David Harmer

If I'm Seen at Halloween, Watch Out!

It's rubbish now at Halloween
Look out there, see what I mean?

Crowds of kids, what a sight
I'm the ghost, tonight's my night.

Silly costumes, witches' hats
Plastic spiders, rubber bats.

No room to breathe because of you
Not that breathing's what I do.

I just can't scare you, I'm a joke
Not a ghastly, ghostly bloke.

When I go BOO to drive you mad
You simply think I'm someone's dad.

Pull out my eyes to make you sick
You all shout 'What a trick!'

I float two metres off the floor
You just yell 'Give us more!'

I groan and moan, shake my chain
You all cry 'Again, again!'

It's not fair, I just can't win
I think I might as well join in.

I'll pretend to trick or treat
You might see me on your street.

But when I give your door a knock
You're going to get a real shock.

You see, my friends, I'm for real
Full of scary spook appeal.

A walking nightmare, then you'll see
What happens when you mess with me.

David Harmer

Bone-Fire Night

Tonight's the night to burn so bright
Tonight's the night to set alight
Racked up, stacked bones so white
Bones on fire – Bone-Fire Night

Every monster can delight
Every creature loves the sight
Piled up to the highest height
Bones on fire – Bone-Fire Night

Skulls and spines, fingers, feet
All picked clean of flesh and meat
Nothing left to taste or eat
Watch them crackle in the heat

Jigsaw skeletons ignite
Exploding just like dynamite
Splinter in the flaming light
Bones on fire – Bone-Fire Night

Paul Cookson

The Sockodile

It does not live in swamps or mud
But on boys' bedroom floors
Camouflaged with woolly skin
That covers up those jaws
It preys upon unwitting feet
With hidden needle smile
The ankle biting, pain inciting
Blood delighting Sockodile

Lying still for days and weeks
Waiting for a treat
The silence leads to violence
And the taste of sweaty feet
Solitary, predatory
Hunting all the while
The snipping snapping, flipping flapping
Tendon trapping Sockodile

Paul Cookson

The Mist, the Fog
and the Big Black Dog

Don't go to the moors at midnight
Don't go to the moors alone
The mist, the fog and the big black dog
Will chill you to the bone

You can hear the growling rumble
You can hear the guttural sound
In the mist and fog, the big black dog
Is prowling round and round

Its fur is spiked with brambles
Its paws are cloaked with mud
In the mist, the fog, the big black dog
Has nostrils scenting blood

A tongue so long and steaming
A tongue so rank and dripping
In the mist and fog, the big black dog
Licks fangs designed for ripping

Too many teeth that crowd that mouth
Too many angles jutting
In the mist and the fog, the big black dog's
Incisors primed for cutting

Crimson eyes of menace
Crimson eyes aglow
In the mist and fog, the big black dog
Is following where you go
Wherever you may go
Wherever you may goooooooooooooooooooooooooo

Paul Cookson

Teachers After Dark

Tonight I took my dog
Towards the local park
Like a fool, I walked past school
As it was getting dark.

Bushes were in shadow
Mist curled on the ground
The moon's first rays cut through the haze
I heard a hissing sound.

That was when I saw him
He lifted up his head
A nasty bloke in a long black cloak
I'll tell you what he said.

'By day I am your teacher
At night that's not so true
It's really good this taste for blood
So come and meet my crew!'

Another twenty vampires
All set for dark adventures
Materialized before my eyes
And opened wide their dentures.

What a fearful sight
These cruel, demented creatures
Howled with grief, gnashed their teeth
And all of them were teachers!

By now I'd had enough
So I unleashed the dog
The horrid gang's loathsome fangs
Vanished in the fog.

But they're out there somewhere
Believe me, I'm no liar
And our dear Sir is their leader
A fully fanged vampire!

David Harmer

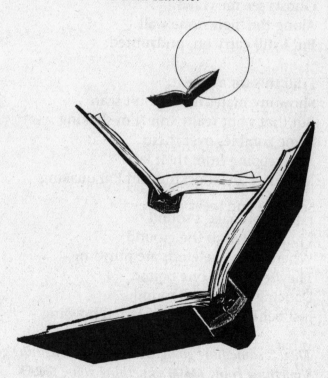

Hocus-Pocus Hall

*There's something going **BOO** there's something going **EEK***
*Something going **AAAGH** something going **SHRIEK***
*Something going **WHOO** feel my stomach quiver*
*Something going **HA HA HA**, a real shiver-giver.*

The evening shadows fall
On Hocus-Pocus Hall
Which everybody knows is haunted
Ghosts see me crawl
Along the high stone wall
But I still carry on, undaunted.

I did this for a dare
Show my mates that I don't scare
But that's not really true, I'm shaking
Some zombies over there
Are creeping from their lair
My knees are knocking and I'm quaking.

I dare not make a sound
I jump down to the ground
Where bony skeletons are prowling
They're over in one bound
Dancing round and round
Just behind a banshee's started howling.

*There's something going **BOO** there's something going **EEK***
*Something going **AAAGH** something going **SHRIEK***
*Something going **WHOO** feel my stomach quiver*
*Something going **HA HA HA**, a real shiver-giver.*

Skinny skeletons clutch my sleeve
You won't leave, you won't leave
Ghosts are screaming from the towers
Now you're ours, now you're ours
Nightmares whisper down my ear
You must stay forever here.

*There's something going **BOO** there's something going **EEK***
*Something going **AAAGH** something going **SHRIEK***
*Something going **WHOO** feel my stomach quiver*
*Something going **HA HA HA**, a real shiver-giver.*

I need to run away
Find all my friends today
But nettles and thistle leaves are growing
And all these voices say
This is where I have to stay
Thickening ivy's going to stop me going.

I'm pinned down on a stone
And I am not alone
The demon on my chest is grinning
So I start to groan
Then begin to moan
My poor thumping head is spinning.

So if you come to see
What happened here to me
The day that I made my fateful call
You will always be
Trapped here eternally
In the haunted grounds of Hocus-Pocus Hall.

And we'll be going **BOO** and we'll be going **EEK**
We'll be going **AAAGH** we'll be going **SHRIEK**
We'll be going **WHOO** feel your stomach quiver
We'll be going **HA HA HA**, a real shiver-giver.

David Harmer

Four Films I Do Not Want to See

Zombie Dinner Ladies Cook My Dog!
Dance of the Mutant Vampire Teachers
Alien Baby Nappy Splurge Fest
Death Kiss Suction Grandma Leeches

Paul Cookson

The Thing of the Wild Frontier

Half man, half wolf, half grizzly bear
Half bison, buffalo too
Double the power of any man
And twice the size of you.

Hunchback shuffle on hind legs
It lurches left to right
Cloven hoof and taloned claw
It howls all through the night.

This mutant roams the prairies
It travels far and near
Nothing goes unnoticed
All sound is crystal clear.

The thing's the king, the thing's the king
All sound is crystal clear
Nothing goes unnoticed
To the king of the wild frontier.

The thing's the king, the thing's the king
It knows no bounds or fear
There is no sound that isn't heard
To the king of the wild frontier.

The thing's the king, the thing's the king
There's nothing it can't hear
It listens from its forehead
The king of the wild frontier.

The thing's the king, the thing's the king
All sound is crystal clear
It listens from its forehead
The thing of the wild . . . front . . . ear.

Paul Cookson

There's a Monster in the Garden

If the water in your fishpond fizzes and foams
And there's giant teeth-marks on the plastic gnomes
You've found huge claw prints in the flower-bed
And just caught sight of a two-horned head
Put a stick on your front lawn with a bit of card on
Look out everybody – there's a monster in the garden.

You haven't seen the dustman for several weeks
Haven't seen the gasman, he was looking for leaks
Haven't seen the paper girl, postman or plumber
Haven't seen the window-cleaner since last summer
Don't mean to be nosy, I do beg your pardon
Look out everybody – there's a monster in the garden.

Monster monster ooh there's a monster
> *Eat you eat you GULP it'll eat you*
> *Bite you bite you CRUNCH it'll bite you*

Scare you scare you WOW it'll scare you
Snog you snog you UGH it'll snog you
Look out everybody
There's a monster in the garden.

One dark night it'll move in downstairs
Start living in the kitchen, take you unawares
Frighten you, bite on you, with howls and roars
It'll crash and smash about, push you out of doors
In the cold and snow the ice and rain will harden
Look out everybody – there's a monster in the garden.

Now listen to me neighbour, all of this is true
It happened next door, now it's happening to you
There's something nasty on the compost heap
Spends all day there curled up asleep
You don't want your bones crunched or jarred on
Look out everybody – there's a monster in the garden.

David Harmer

Bath Waters Run Deep

Dad did not smile nor did he laugh
Seeing the shark-fin in the bath
Instead, began to fuss and fuss
When tickled by the octopus
His eyes could not believe it real
The shock of the electric eel
And then up popped the toilet lid
Shooting out a giant squid
His arms and legs began to flail
Until he saw the killer whale
He sat stock still, too scared to move
The swordfish had a point to prove
It did so with a sharpened swish
And then Dad saw the jellyfish
That shivered, shook and grew and grew
So Dad began to shiver too
That was the least of current troubles
When bursting upwards through the bubbles
A mile of oily coils and – yes
It was the monster from Loch Ness!
Dad wished he washed in just the sink
Bath water's deeper than you think
He also wished – and this is rude
He was not bathing in the nude
And since he was, his final wish
Was not to see piranha fish
Alas, these wishes don't come true
Piranha fish swam into view
A thousand spiky snapping teeth
That started biting underneath

A starfish then joined in the fun
At this point Dad began to run
So out he leaped with piercing howl
But could not find a single towel
A blur of pink and he was gone
Crabs and lobsters hanging on
So when you have a bath take care
Of monsters lurking everywhere
The moral of this tale will be
It's safer bathing in the sea!

Paul Cookson

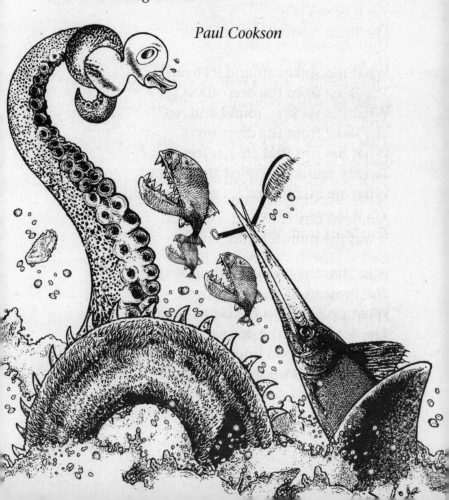

The Beast from the Deep Abyss

What lives in a watery grave?
The Beast from the deep abyss.
What's emerging from the waves?
The Beast from the deep abyss.
What is slippery? What is slimy?
What has scales so green and shiny?
What has seaweed cold and grimy?
Yes it is, yes it is . . .
The Beast from the deep abyss.

What has spikes around its head?
The Beast from the deep abyss.
What has suckers, round and red?
The Beast from the deep abyss.
What has fins that are ten feet long?
Twenty tentacles, coiled and strong?
What ate Moby Dick . . . and then King Kong?
Yes it is, yes it is . . .
The Beast from the deep abyss.

What has the teeth of a thousand sharks?
The Beast from the deep abyss.
What gave the electric eel its sparks?
The Beast from the deep abyss.
What sucks blood from living creatures?
Looks for prey upon the beaches?
What's so foul it eats up teachers?
With a slobbery, blubbery, rubbery kiss

Yes it is, yes it is . . .
The Beast from the deep,
The Beast from the deep,
The Beast from the deep abyss

Paul Cookson

Grandma's Bag

Leathery hide
Zipped teeth
Things disappear when it is near

Eyeless – not blind
Unseeing – but knowing
Senses when things are close

Patiently – it waits
Evilly – it lingers
Hungrily – it knows when times are right

At first it was a glove here
Or a sweet wrapper there
Last week it managed to get a whole frozen chicken

Today the dog won't go near it
The cat stays well away
And when the baby crawled right past it

I'm sure I saw it move . . .

Paul Cookson

What Is It?

Got a monster in my matchbox
It isn't very big
Nose like a crocodile
Face like a pig
Wings like a penguin
Teeth like a stoat
Sings like a croaking crow
Stinks like a goat
Don't know what it is
Don't really care
Just look inside my matchbox
Yes it's still there.

David Harmer

The Midnight Sprite

As it flies at midnight
It starts to blow its fuses
Horridness that steams
Nastiness that oozes

It creeps around in darkness
And plays its naughty game
Damaging your bedroom
And you get all the blame

Dinting all the walls
With its magic power
Throwing all your toys around
And blocking up the shower

As it rants and rages
All throughout the night
You never know it's there
The evil Midnight Sprite

Daisy Cookson and Paul Cookson

On the Bus

The woman on the bus looked normal
Nobody noticed her except me
I saw her look at the buzzing fly
She watched it land on the window

And then when she thought no one was looking
Her eyelids closed and her mouth unhinged
As silent and whip-like the tongue unfurled
And the fly was no more

It was over in the blink of an eye
And then her own eyelids slowly opened
And she saw me watching so she smiled and nodded
While winking one reptilian golden eye

Paul Cookson

Next Door

My mum says
The woman next door
Isn't a fly.

A huge bluebottle
Rubbing six thin legs together
Crawling upside down on the ceiling
Sticking her long nose into the jam.

My mum says
That buzzing and whirring and humming
We hear each day through the wall
Is only a Hoover.

If that's true, why
Does her husband scuttle
Over the floor on eight hairy legs
And build thick webs
In the dark cupboard under the stairs?

And why does Stan
Her eldest son
Buy huge cans of Deadly Flykill?

When I next see her
Zooming over the compost and dustbins
I'll have to ask her
Just what's SWAT!

David Harmer

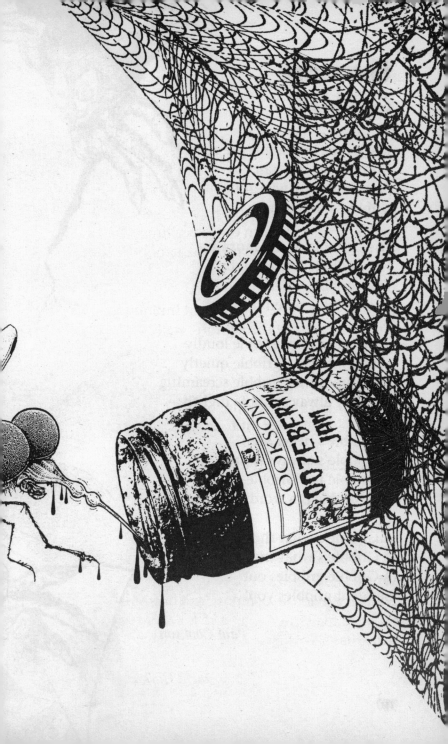

There Are Gribbles

There are Gribbles in the attic
Gribbles on the stair
Gribbles in my wardrobe
Gribbles everywhere.

They gribble in the morning
They gribble late at night
They gribble when it's dark
They gribble when it's light.

Sometimes they gribble loudly
Sometimes they gribble quietly
Sometimes they gribble screaming
But they always gribble nightly.

A Gribble's never seen
A Gribble's always heard
A Gribble is a Gribble
Is a Gribble is a word.

A Gribble's what they are
A Gribble's what they do
A Gribble gribbles out
Before it gribbles you!

Paul Cookson

Phew!

Something's outside our tent
A slithery, snuffling noise
I don't know what it is
But I know that it eats boys.

Something's outside our tent
I bet it's big and hairy
With chomping jaws and bulging eyes
Looking very scary.

Something's outside our tent
It's grunting and its near
Sounds like it could freeze my blood
Keep it out of here!

Something's outside our tent
I hope it's gone by morning.
Wait a tick, it's next door's tent
It's only Darren snoring!

David Harmer

Dracula's Complaint

You'd look poorly, you'd look pale
Skin all deathly shades of grey
You'd look sickly, you'd look frail
Stuck in a coffin in a grave all day.

Go for a shave, can't see my face
Spend half my life dressed as a bat
Living all my days at subnormal pace
With these enormous teeth, who needs that?

Night after night I ride my bike
Looking around for a bite to eat
Living in a graveyard isn't what I like
The neighbours howl, their breath's not sweet.

I'm bored stiff, it's a pain in the neck
Living in the ground, cold and damp
I'm turning into a Transylvanian wreck
My whole life needs a thorough revamp.

I look in the paper, read the small ads
I need a new job, need a fresh start
I want to escape the curse of the Vlads
Try to do that with a stake through your heart.

David Harmer

Walls Have Eyes

Some say that walls have ears
But they are telling lies
Walls do not have ears
Because the walls have eyes

Hiding in the patterns
Camouflaged disguise
Lurking in the curtains
The walls around have eyes

Opening and closing
Every shape and size
Devil dark demonic
All the walls have eyes

Unblinking and unwinking
These watching waiting spies
Are nightmare staring glaring
Scaring walls with eyes

Nasty and nocturnal
The walls that terrorize
Blighted by the night
That has a thousand eyes

Paul Cookson

Don't Muck About with Giants

I can hear the heavy beat
Of his footsteps far away
I can feel the earthquake shaking
As he stomps my way today

Thump-thump-thumperty thump

Thump-thump-thumperty thump

I can hear his groans and grunts
As he marches down the hill
I can hear his grumpy grumble
Getting clearer, nearer still

Thump-thump-thumperty thump

Thump-thump-thumperty thump

I can see his big brown boots
His revolting hairy knees
He is almost here upon me
Taller than the tallest trees

Thump-thump-thumperty thump

Thump-thump-thumperty thump

I can smell his stinky socks
And his foul, disgusting breath
I can hear his chomping teeth
He will frighten me to death!

Thump-thump-thumperty thump

Thump-thump-thumperty thump

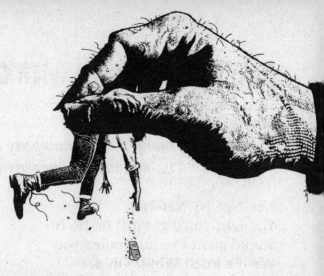

I hear his horrid laughter
As he smacks his greasy lips
Slaver dribbles down his beard
He wants me with double chips!
> *Thump-thump-thumperty thump*
> *Thump-thump-thumperty thump*

Now I think I'm going to scream
Sick with fear and terrified
He's so hungry he will eat me
Mashed or boiled or fried
> *Thump-thump-thumperty thump*
> *Thump-thump-thumperty thump*

Watch me hide behind this tree
He's not seen me after all
Look he's walking round the corner
Disappeared behind that wall
> *Thump-thump-thumperty thump*
> *Thump-thump-thumperty thump*

Yes I think he's really gone
And at last I'm safe and free
I'll celebrate straight away
Big fat giant, can't catch me!

> *Thump-thump-thumperty thump*
> *Thump-thump-thumperty thump*

Ner–Ner–Ni–Ner–Ner
Thought you'd got me, ho ho ho
Stupid giant I've just fooled you
What a loser! What? Oh no!

> *Thump-thump-thumperty thump*
> *Thump-thump-thumperty thump*

He heard me calling names
See, he's turning round to stare
Hear him growl and gnash his teeth
Yikes he's back! Just over there!

> *Thump-thump-thumperty thump*
> *Thump-thump-thumperty thump*

Time to run now for your life
Don't mock giants please, it's true
They will grind your bones to powder
I'd run too if I were you!!!!!!!!!!!!!

Thump-thump-thumperty thump
Thump-thump-thumperty thump
CRUNCH!

David Harmer

The Footprint

Bigger than Brother's
Wider than Mother's
And twice as long as Dad's
The footprint

Part hoof, part paw
Part hand, part claw
From another world
The footprint

Outside my window
That close
Larger than life
And invisible as death

The worst thing was
It was just the one
Solitary and predatory
Footprint

No, the worst thing was this . . .

It was burned into the concrete
Deep and solid
Scorched and eternal
The menacing evidence
That was . . .

The footprint

Paul Cookson

The Hunter and the Hunted

With skies as black as treacle
Save for a full skull moon
A perfect cloak of darkness
For the dreaded vampire flying
The dreaded vampire flying
In search of a rose red bloom
The rose red blood tide bloom

With the midnight hour of menace
No earthly powers resist
The hunter and the hunted
Defenceless necks lie open
Defenceless necks lie open
Awaiting their last kiss
The grinning vampire kiss

With dark romance and murder
The long dead cherish breath
Gaze greedily at innocence
Where sleep and dreams are previews
Sleep and dreams are previews
Of a deep dark nightmare death
Damned eternal death

Those jagged canine razor blades
Stiletto points of pain
Evil beauty glinting
Preparing for the sacrifice
The dark unholy sacrifice
Of life and loss and gain
Life and loss and gain

The hideous monstrosity
No truth or beauty in this beast
Just soulless empty vessels
Addicts to affliction
Addicts to affliction
Who crave that crimson feast
That crimson harvest feast

Paul Cookson

A Million Muddy Monsters

A million muddy monsters
Sliding in the sludge
A million muddy monsters
In mud as thick as fudge

A million muddy monsters
Sploshing in the puddles
A million muddy monsters
Making mess and muddles

A million muddy monsters
Jumping, thumping
Charging, barging
Bashing, crashing
Rolling, strolling

In icky-sticky
Ooopy-gloopy
Yukky-mucky
Sloppy-gloppy
Chunky-gunky
Ooooey-gooey
SPLOPDOSHY MUD!

A million muddy monsters
Slopping in the slime
A million muddy monsters
Having a great time

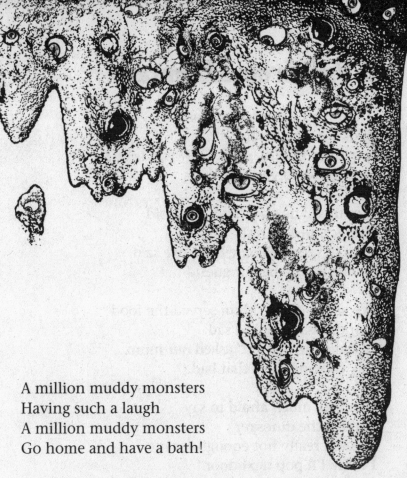

A million muddy monsters
Having such a laugh
A million muddy monsters
Go home and have a bath!

David Harmer

A Visit from a Dinosaur

A dinosaur came to our door
Looking for a meal
We asked him in, said, 'How you been?
How good do you feel?'

'I'm tired,' he said, 'and very cold
Hungry, need a rest.'
'You're very welcome here,' we said
'Come in and be our guest.'

We all sat down, Mum served the food
Our dinosaur looked sad
'What's the matter?' asked our mum
'My cooking's not that bad.'

'I'm very much afraid to say,'
Replied the dinosaur
'There's really not enough for me
I think I'll pop next door.'

'You see,' he said, 'I feel so thin
I mustn't get much thinner
But your neighbours seem quite plump
That's where I'll have my dinner.'

We heard the yells, we heard the screams
We didn't pay much heed
But sad to say our dinosaur
Had gone next door to feed.

He came back up our garden path
His mouth was full of bones
'Very toothsome, very sweet,'
He said in cheerful tones.

'Don't think us rude but we're not food,'
We shouted through the door
'Now go away without delay
Bother us no more.'

He burped and waved, he growled, 'Goodbye.'
Set off down the lane
And we made sure no dinosaur
Came round here again.

David Harmer

A Dragon's Breath

Scorched earth
Singed bone
Acrid smoke
Brimstone

Molten lava
Soot and ash
Thunderbolt
Lightning flash

Mouldering cinders
Long dead trees
A dragon's breath
Can smell of these

The stench of death
Through and through
Living breathing
Barbecue

Paul Cookson

Dragon Danger!

When the dragon comes down
Going to be a lot of trouble
When the dragon comes down
Going to be a lot of heat
When the dragon comes down
Going to hear some rumbling thunder
When the dragon comes down
Going to knock you off your feet
*When the dragon comes **down**!*

No good hiding in the castle
No good hiding in the keep
No good hiding in the dungeons
In the cellars or in the rubbish heap.

No good hiding in your houses
No good hiding behind doors
No good hiding under tables
In cupboards or underneath the floors.

No good hiding in the river
No good hiding in the hills
No good hiding in the forests
He'll get you with his fire-breathing skills.

Chorus

The dragon is raging, maddened and mean
The nastiest dragon you've ever seen
Some knight stole his treasure, then his princess
Now he feels angry, confessing distress.

Chorus

No good heading for the tower
No good heading for the roof
No good heading for the shower
You're kidding if you think it's fireproof.

No good heading for the mountains
No good heading for the lake
No good heading for the seaside
His bone-crunching jaws will make you ache.

No good heading for the station
No good heading for a train
No good heading for the distance
His mighty claws will grab you once again.

Chorus

He wants his revenge, fire bursts from his mouth
He flies to the north, the west and the south
He flies to the east, he's shooting out flames
He's on the rampage, he's not playing games.

Chorus

David Harmer

The Bearded Dragon

The crickets don't know it
Even the oldest, wisest locust
Has this to learn.

After you've dropped into the heat
Of the scorching light
Hopped over the branches
And through the leaf mould
Something else is waiting for you.

There's no way back
The sky is metal
The world ends in walls of glass
And the drystone skin you're crawling on
Is the head of a lizard.

No raging fires, no mighty wingbeats
Just grey-green scales and thin, hooked claws
A terrible ring of spikes round the neck
And jaws so quick they snap you dead.

After the feeding
The lizard's throat flushes black
She lifts her head, lowers her gaze
Her scaly eyes swivel, then shut.

Somewhere underneath the branches
A single cricket sings to itself.

David Harmer

The Secret Monster

There's a little monster
Living down our street
I take him lots of sausages
And fish and chips to eat.

He's very very scaly
Spotted green and red
Purple wings, orange claws
Horns upon his head.

I climb up on his back
And we start to fly
Zooming up to the stars
Silver in the sky.

Swooping by the moon
Mars and Mercury
My fantastic monster
Just him and me.

Only I can see him
We have loads of fun
He really is a secret
Don't tell anyone!

David Harmer

Grendel

Midnight prowler, death-bringer
A maddened monster, mayhem-monger
Marching out from marsh and moorland
To sniff the scent of men.

Hurling havoc, hard and hurtful
Hollowed out with smoking anger
The gaunt, gruesome, ghastly Grendel
Revenge-wreaker, skull-crusher
Sinew-snapper, muscle-mangler
Bodysnatcher, brain-gouger
Carcass-carver, eyes like fires
Stamps and stifles farm and homestead.

Teeth as jagged as battle-swords
Giant claws ripping rib-bones
Tougher than an iron tree
Reptilian on two great legs
His breath stinks of rotten flesh
His heart stinks of hate and horror.

This is Grendel.

David Harmer

(*Now go and read the poem* **Beowulf***, and find out lots more about this monster.*)

Odysseus and the Cyclops

*(A story from Ancient Greece about the hero
Odysseus and the savage giant Polyphemus)*

Polyphemus was a Cyclops
A giant with one eye
In the middle of his forehead
A most unpleasant guy
He captured Odysseus
Together with his crew
And pretty soon the Cyclops
Was brewing human stew.

But blinded by Odysseus
He found he couldn't keep
All the Greeks escaping
Beneath his giant sheep
Polyphemus cried in agony
'What is your name?'
'Nobody,' said the hero
'And escaping is my game!'

The Cyclops was raging mad
Let out a mighty roar
And all his Cyclops mates
Said, 'What's this roaring for?'
'I'm trying to catch my enemy
That's why I'm furious.'
'What's his name?' 'Nobody.'
'Well, you won't be needing us!'

Odysseus and his crew
Soon slipped away by boat
Polyphemus yelled after them
Anger burning up his throat
'Who are you really
That I can't catch or see?'
'Odysseus,' came the reply
'And you aren't eating me.'

The giant's wrath erupted
He started hurling stones
Trying to sink the Greeks
And crush their living bones
But with every rock he missed
He flung them all in vain
And Polyphemus was left there
With his loneliness and pain.

David Harmer

Mirror Mirror on the Wall

Medusa the Gorgon
Was having a bad hair day.
She couldn't do a thing
With some of the snakes
Others were too sleepy and dozy
To be of any use.
A few of them
Were fizzing and hissing
Spitting venom
With a frenzied energy
That was driving her mad
They coiled, uncoiled, coiled again
And simply wouldn't lie flat.

Medusa the Gorgon
Was in despair.
How could she manage
These distressing tresses?
No good going to the hairdresser
She'd only turn them into stone.
She sighed with frustration
Knowing she'd have to do it herself
So, without thinking,
She reached for her snake-comb
And looked into the mirror.

Whoops!

David Harmer

(*Medusa was one of the three Gorgons, monsters from Greek myths. She was killed by the hero Perseus. She had living snakes on her head instead of hair, and when she stared at you, you turned to stone. My poem changes things a bit as, in a careless moment, she does that to herself.*)

Monsters at the Door

There's a monster at the door
Don't let it in!
There's a monster at the door
Don't let it in!

There's a monster at the door
You can hear its mighty roar
And it wants a tasty snack
So don't you turn your back
Because it wants to chew
On me and then on you.

There's a ghost at the door
Don't let it in!
There's a ghost at the door
Don't let it in!

There's a ghost at the door
Floating from the floor
And it wants to howl and scream
Like a mad, demented dream
It will frighten us to death
With its chilly, icy breath.

There's a vampire at the door
Don't let it in!
There's a vampire at the door
Don't let it in!

There's a vampire at the door
And we can't take much more

See its gleaming, shiny white
Fangs stretching for a bite
Yes it wants a little peck
On the back of my neck.

There's a werewolf at the door
Don't let it in!
There's a werewolf at the door
Don't let it in!

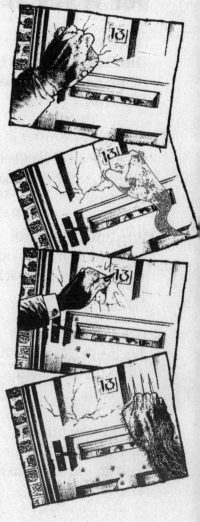

There's a werewolf at the door
With a crooked, curving claw
That's sharper than a spear
Don't let it get in here
It's howling at the moon
Wants its dinner very soon.

There's a monster at the door
Don't let it in!
A ghost at the door
Don't let it in!
A vampire at the door
Don't let it in!
A werewolf at the door
Don't let it in!

DON'T
LET
THEM
IN!

AAAAAAAAAAAAAAAAAAAAGH!

David Harmer

For Whom the Bell Trolls

Down by the park
There's a dirty, dirty brook
He lives there, just beneath the bridge
The Troll

Ugly as sin
Face like an unmade bed
Greedy, scary eyes like marbles in walnuts
The Troll

Wiry, matted beard
Remains of meals and flies and mud
Through a hedge backwards
The Troll

Grimace or grin
Ten teeth, just like the commandments
All of them broken
The Troll

Guards the bridge
By the dirty, dirty brook
And an old-fashioned bell
The Troll

No one can pass
Unless you ring that bell
And wait for the menacing growl of
The Troll

Cross his greasy palms
You can cross his bridge
Pay the toll to the Troll
The Troll Bridge Toll Bridge Troll

Paul Cookson

Do Not Go Down to Loch Ness

Something stirs from way down deep
Something breathing wakes from sleep
Here's a secret you can keep
Here's a truth I must confess
Do not go down to Loch Ness

Black and oily coils and scales
Flippers bigger than a whale's
Fangs and fins, talons, tails
Something more, nothing less
Do not go down to Loch Ness

Hit or myth, truth or fake
Who can hear this kraken wake?
History beneath this lake
Prehistoric – who can guess?
Do not go down to Loch Ness

Do not swim and do not dive
When you feel those currents writhe
Lest you be dragged down alive
Jaws that squeeze, claws that press
Do not go down to Loch Ness

People come from far and near
There's no Highland welcome here
They don't know that they should fear
Coils that tighten and caress
Do not go down to Loch Ness

Stay away, it's for the best
Do not go down to Loch Ness

Paul Cookson

Our School Monster

It sucks the ink from our felt pens
Crunches pencils, guzzles glue
Eats the markers from the whiteboards
Sometimes eats the whiteboards too.

It hides inside the PE store
Makes a dreadful mess and then
Sinks its teeth into the footballs
Making sure they're flat again.

It snuffles crisps and snaffles sweets
Scatters litter on the yard
Rips the towels in the toilets
Just look out, be on your guard.

Just because you haven't seen it
Doesn't mean it isn't there
Just because you don't believe me
Doesn't mean you mustn't care.

It's the monster in our school
You will see great pools of drool
Slobber from its giant jaws
As it stalks the corridors.
Look in cupboards, under stairs
Behind bookshelves, behind chairs
It's there all right, it's not nice
So just you heed my kind advice.

Just because you haven't seen it
Doesn't mean it isn't there
Just because you don't believe me
Doesn't mean you mustn't care.

It trips the school alarms at night
Our poor caretaker gets no sleep
Frightens all the dinner ladies
With its silent, prowling creep.

Our computers all go mad
It roars with glee as they crash
Then it chews the registers
And swallows all the petty cash.

One day you'll feel its burning breath
On your neck and so you'll turn
See its giant, gruesome features
That's perhaps when you will learn.

Just because you haven't seen it
Doesn't mean it isn't there
Just because you don't believe me
Doesn't mean you mustn't care.

David Harmer

REGISTER
Record of Enrolment & Attendance
Teacher: Mr.W.Wolfe
Class: F3
House: Hammer
Bogsnorts School

Mason the Moody Monster

Mason the moody monster
Was in a gloomy mood
He wasn't feeling happy
A really dismal dude.

He stuck out his tongue
Like all small boys
Tugged at his ears
Made a rude noise
Shouted 'Knickers!'
Pulled a face
Stomped and stamped
All over the place
Threw his dinner at the wall
Began to bellow, burp and bawl
Growled and grunted
Kicked a chair
Slammed a door
Screamed 'IT'S NOT FAIR!'

Yes Mason the moody monster
Was having a terrible day
And his lumpy-grumpy feelings
Would not go away.

But his dad sang a song
And his mum cracked a joke
They tickled his tummy
They gave him a poke
They let him play football
And he scored

He did a small dance
And he wasn't so bored
And then he chuckled
Twinkled his toes
Scratched at his head
Poked at his nose
He hopped and he skipped
Drank some pop
Started to smile
And he couldn't stop.

Then Mason the moody monster
Laughed out loud with a roar
And Mason the moody monster
Wasn't moody any more.

David Harmer

Sir Guy and the Enchanted Princess

Through howling winds on a storm-tossed moor
Sir Guy came to a castle door.

He was led by some strange power
To the deepest dungeon of a ruined tower.

A Princess sat on a jewelled throne
Her lovely features carved in stone.

His body trembled, was she dead?
Then her sweet voice filled his head.

'These evil spirits guard me well
Brave Sir Knight, please break their spell.

Though I am stone, you shall see
Kiss me once, I shall be free.'

As demons howled she came to life
Blushed and whispered 'Have you a wife?'

'My love' he said 'still remains
With collecting stamps and spotting trains.

But as long as you do as you're told
I think you'll do, come on it's cold.'

'Oh' she cried 'you weedy bore
I wish I was entranced once more.'

Lightning struck, the demons hissed
Sir Guy was stone, a voice croaked 'Missed!'

The Princess rode his horse away
And poor Sir Guy's still there today.

David Harmer

The Visitor

It was late last night I'm certain
that I saw my bedroom curtain
twitch and flutter
felt a chill, heard him mutter
'Hullo lad I'm back.'

Uncle Jack!
Dead since this time last year.
A pickled onion in his beer
stopped his breath
a sudden death
that sadly took us by surprise.

But there he was, those eyes
one grey, one blue
one through
which the light could pass
the other, glass.

He drifted down, swam about
in his brown suit, flat cap, stout
boots and tie.
I saw him take out his eye.

'It's not a dream
this' he said 'don't scream
I'll not come back, I shan't return.'
Then I felt the ice-cold burn
of his glass eye upon my skin.

Saw his ghastly, ghostly grin
'Don't worry, don't get in a stew
just thought I'd keep an eye on you.'

When I woke up today
I saw the blue eye, not the grey
but when I picked it up to go
it drained away like melting snow.
Didn't it?

David Harmer

The Mudditch

The Mudditch lies below the ground
Submerged beneath the ooze
Makes a hungry crunching sound
When chewing on your shoes

In the cloying clutches stuck
First it bites your toes
Drags you down and eats you up
And as you shrink – it grows

The Mudditch grows . . . and grows

Paul Cookson

We All Have a Monster of Our Own

A monster lives
Deep inside me
It feeds on greed
Drinks down anger
Thrives on shouting
And unkind words.

When it escapes
It attacks
The people I love
Scars and scares my family
Lashes its tail
In the face of my friends.

I see the horror
As they recoil
From its poison
I try to fight it
Hammer back
The bars of its cage
Even though
It bites and bites.

It's always there
A rumbling dragon
Curled asleep
In the glow of its fires
Waiting to wake.

David Harmer

The Monster Spider on the Ceiling

Watching, waiting, way up high
Loitering with evil eye
For that moment of revealing
The monster spider on the ceiling

Pupils sitting in the hall
Assemble while it starts to crawl
Step by step, most unappealing
The monster spider on the ceiling

Like a dark cloud in the blue
Eventually comes into view
There's no hiding or concealing
The monster spider on the ceiling

One by one, all realize
With open mouths and widened eyes
Pointing, panicking and squealing
The monster spider on the ceiling

Shrieking, shouting as it's crawling
Frightened that it may start falling
The assembled trembled, senses reeling
The monster spider on the ceiling

To the rescue, one brave teacher
On a chair reached to the creature
Very soon she was dealing
With that monster on the ceiling

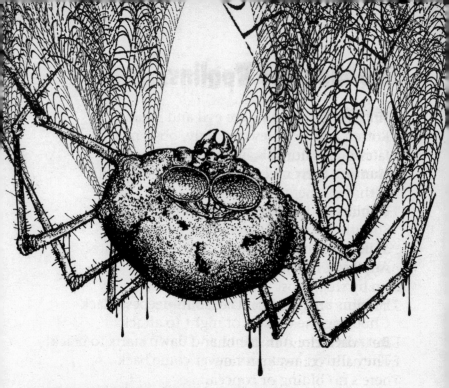

With a pint glass from the staffroom
And some cardboard from the classroom
One swift move and she was peeling
The monster spider from the ceiling

Safely, soundly, slowly, surely
The creepy caught by Mrs Crawley
She relieved all anxious feeling
Caught the monster from the ceiling

Took it out across the yard
To the fence and chucked it hard
Somersaulting and cartwheeling
Bye bye spider from the ceiling!

Paul Cookson

Hoblins and Boglins

Hoblins and Boglins are evil and mean
Rotten and troublesome, ugly, obscene
Horrid and horrible, manic and green
Planting their nightmares into your dream

Hoblins and Boglins are poison and spite
Shouting out lies in your ears late at night
Making up monsters and creatures that bite
Anything nasty to give you a fright

Hoblins and Boglins have souls deepest black
Choosing the darkest of night to attack
But when the sun shines and dawn starts to crack
They shrivel away and never come back

Until midnight strikes and daylight has gone
The Hoblins and Boglins are creeping out from
The shadows of shadows to wreak havoc on
The innocent daughter and carefree young son

For Hoblins and Boglins are evil and mean
Rotten and troublesome, ugly, obscene
Horrid and horrible, manic and green
They muffle your mouth and silence your scream

Yes Hoblins and Boglins are poison and spite
Embracing the wrong and loathing the right
Hating the daytime, loving the night
They breathe in the dark and choke in the light

Paul Cookson

Shadowans

Shadowans are shape-shifters
Gliding through the night
Melting with the darkness
Squeezing out the light

Shadowans are silent
Never make a sound
Malevolent and liquid
Blackness spreads around

Shadowans are changelings
A wide-awake nightmare
You can't escape the Shadowans
Lurking everywhere

Paul Cookson

Behind You

Look out – BEHIND YOU
Look out – BEHIND YOU
Look out – BEHIND YOU
The beast is gonna find you

Watching – BEHIND YOU
Waiting – BEHIND YOU
Walking – BEHIND YOU
The beast is gonna find you

Daytime and night-time
The wrong time, the right time
Stay out of sight time
It's looking for a bite time

Watching – BEHIND YOU
Waiting – BEHIND YOU
Walking – BEHIND YOU
The beast is gonna find you

I know and you know
You go fast and go slow
In sunshine and shadow
It follows where you go

Watching – BEHIND YOU
Waiting – BEHIND YOU
Walking – BEHIND YOU
The beast is gonna find you

Crawling and creeping
Sniping and sneaking

Spying and peeping
Hiding and seeking

Watching – BEHIND YOU
Waiting – BEHIND YOU
Walking – BEHIND YOU
The beast is gonna find you

The noises it's making
The scratching and scraping
You're quaking and shaking
Cos there is no escaping

Watching – BEHIND YOU
Waiting – BEHIND YOU
Walking – BEHIND YOU
The beast is gonna find you

So, let me remind you
Let me remind you
Let me remind you
The beast is gonna find you

Look out – BEHIND YOU
Look out – BEHIND YOU
Look out – BEHIND YOU
The beast is gonna find you

Watching – BEHIND YOU
Waiting – BEHIND YOU
Walking – BEHIND YOU
The beast is gonna find you

Paul Cookson